Hidden Picture Scavenger Hunt

ICONIC AMERICAN LANDMARKS

Search & Find The Hidden Objects

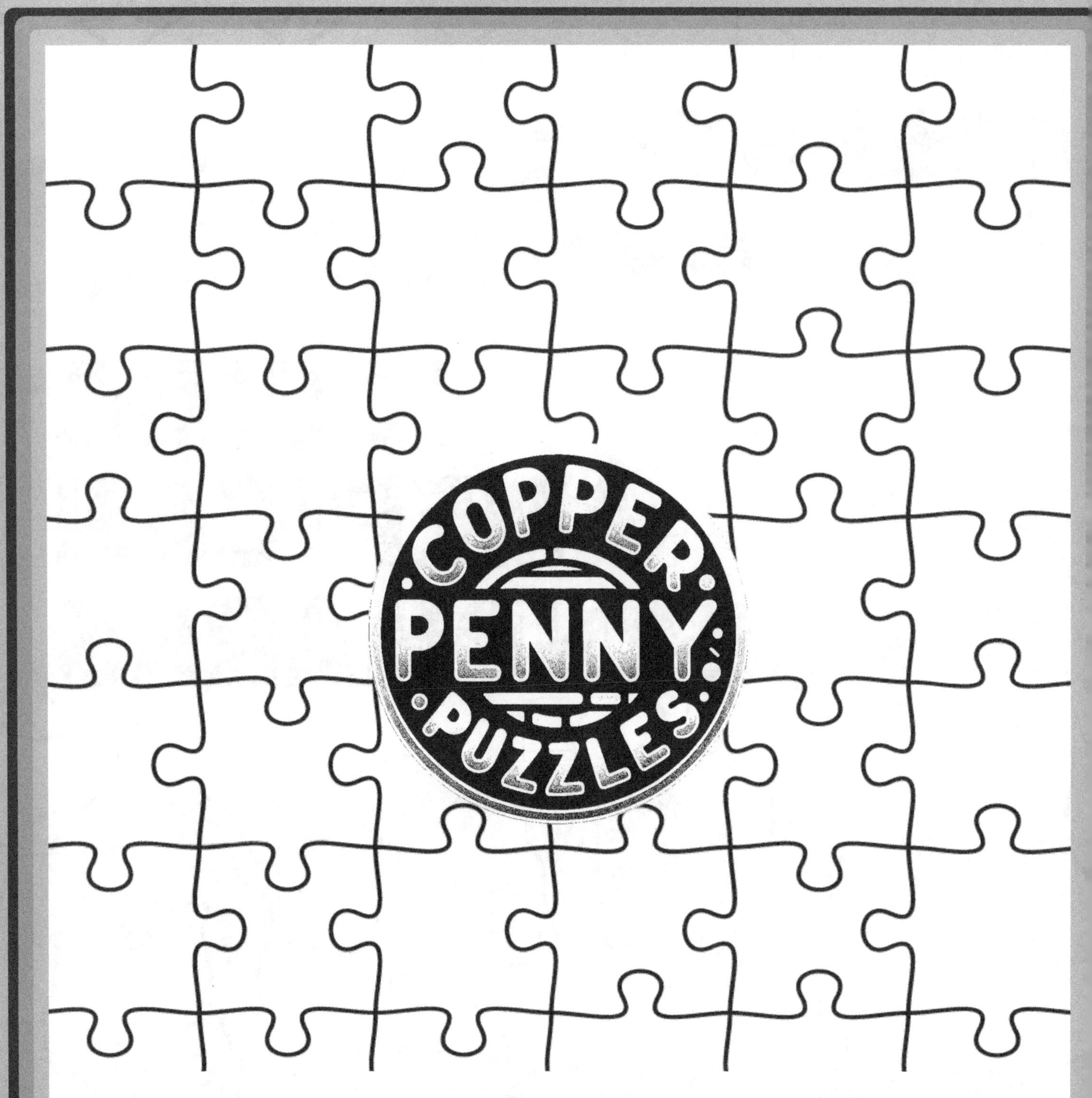
COPPER
PENNY
PUZZLES

HOW TO SOLVE THE PUZZLES

This hidden picture activity book has 31 USA landmark-themed puzzles each with its own scavenger's checklist of 12 clues. Each puzzle has twelve items to search for in a landmark scene. Each scene is a not a photo of the landmark but a **depiction**. Look for stars & stripes, ships, cacti, animals and more - it depends on the puzzle. All the clues are on the left-hand pages with the puzzles on the right. There are checkboxes under each clue so you can check them off as you find each item. All scenes are different and the solutions foe each puzzle are at the back of the book. As an extra bonus, there is a brief description of each landmark and you can color all the scenes, too. Below are two examples. Have fun!

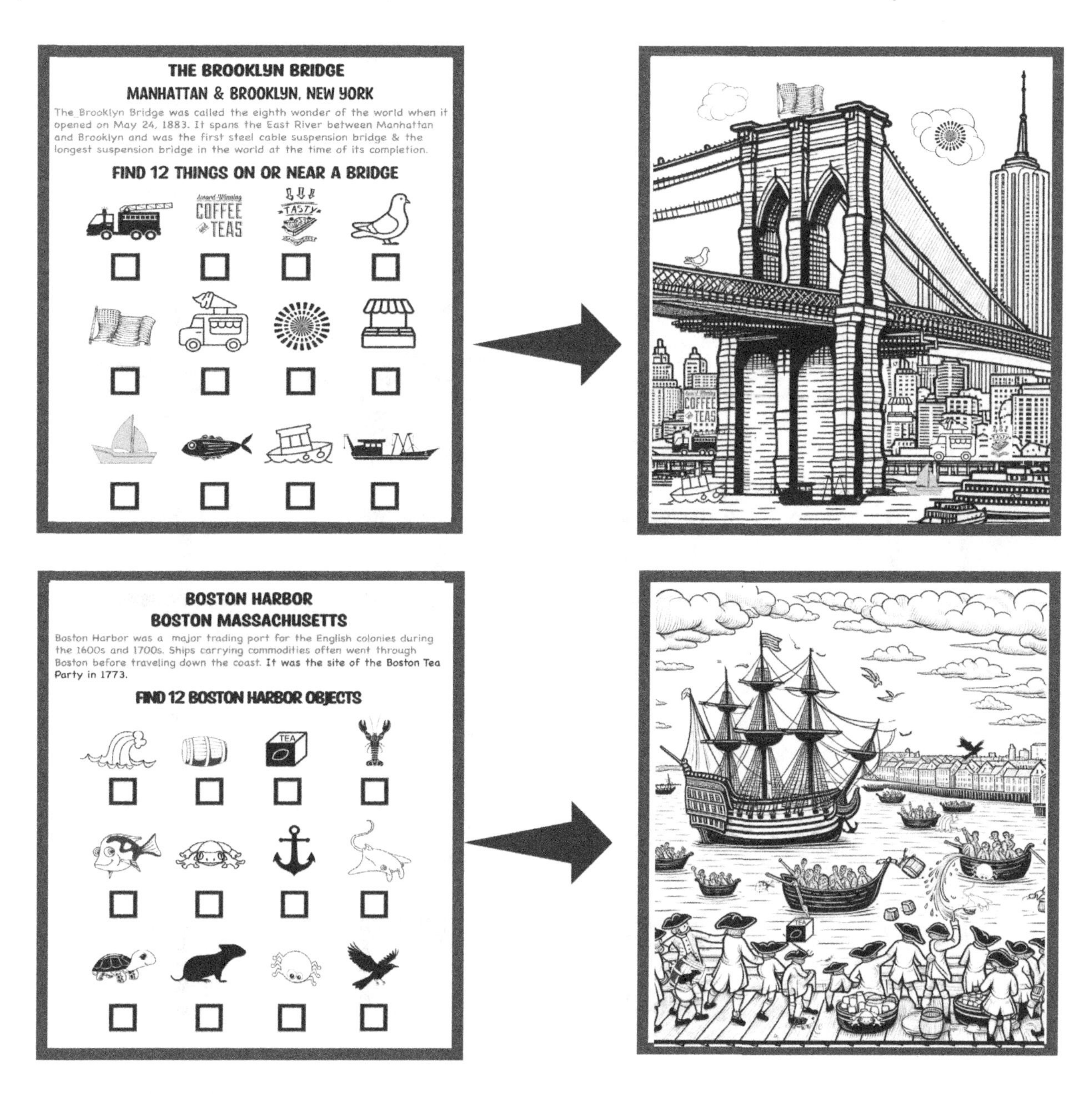

THE STATUE OF LIBERTY
NEW YORK HARBOR

The "Statue of Liberty Enlightening the World" was dedicated October 28, 1886. She's a copper statue of the figure of Libertas, the Roman goddess of Liberty and was a gift of friendship to the U.S. from the people of France. She holds a torch above her head with her right hand and in her left hand is a tablet inscribed July 4, 1776 in Roman numerals. There's a broken chain and shackle at her feet, commemorating the abolition of slavery following the Civil War.

FIND 12 OBJECTS ON LIBERTY ISLAND

Solution on page 67

YOSEMITE NATIONAL PARK

CENTRAL CALIFORNIA

Located in California's Sierra Nevada mountains, Yosemite includes nearly 1,200 square miles of mountainous scenery, including high granite cliffs, waterfalls, ancient giant sequoia trees and expansive wilderness.. First protected in 1864,, millions of people visit each year.

FIND 12 ANIMALS & CAMPING GEAR

Solution on page 67

EARLY AMERICAN FARMHOUSE KITCHEN

Early American farmhouses were simply built with wooden clapboard siding and sitting on flat land. Many had porches that also served as outdoor storage. Being close to water was important so farmhouses were often next to lakes or rivers. During Colonial times the settlers brought Cape Cod and Colonial styles to the east coast because these designs were easily built by hand. They spread west in the 1700s.

FIND 12 KITCHEN ITEMS

Solution on page 67

FARMHOUSE
COOKIES
SUGAR
FLOUR

HOLLYWOOD SIGN

HOLLYWOOD, LOS ANGELES, CALIFORNIA

Originally Hollywoodland, the sign is situated in an area of the Santa Monica mountains. It spells out the word "Hollywood" in 50-foot-tall white uppercase letters. Originally erected in 1923 as an advertisement for a local real estate company, with increasing recognition the sign was left up and replaced with a more durable steel 45-foot-tall sign in 1978.

FIND 12 INSECTS & CRITTERS

Solution on page 67

HOLLYWOOD

LAS VEGAS STRIP
LAS VEGAS, NEVADA

The 4.2 mile Las Vegas Strip, officially Las Vegas Boulevard, is home to the most famous hotels and casinos in the city. The Strip is one of the most popular and iconic tourist destinations in the world, a major contributor to the Las Vegas economy and is well known for its casinos, lounges, showrooms, theaters and nightclubs

FIND 12 DICE, POKER CHIPS & PLAYING CARDS

Solution on page 68

PORTLAND HEAD LIGHT
CAPE ELIZABETH, MAINE

Portland Head Light, an historic lighthouse, sits at the entrance of the main shipping channel into Portland Harbor. Construction started in 1787 at the directive of George Washington and it was completed in 1791. The US Coast Guard maintains the light station, tower, beacon & foghorn.

FIND 12 LIGHTHOUSE OBJECTS

Solution on page 68

NIAGARA FALLS

NIAGARA FALLS, NEW YORK

The Falls were formed from glacial-melt 12,000 years ago. Established in 1885 as Niagara Reservation, Niagara Falls is America's oldest state park. There are actually three Falls & they're in the US and Canada. The world's first hydroelectric power plant was created in Niagara Falls in 1885 and supplies more than ¼ of the power in New York State and Ontario, Canada.

FIND 12 WATERFALL OBJECTS

Solution on page 68

BOSTON HARBOR
BOSTON, MASSACHUSETTS

Boston Harbor was a major trading port for the English colonies during the 1600s and 1700s. Ships carrying commodities often went through Boston before traveling down the coast. It was the site of the Boston Tea Party in 1773.

FIND 12 BOSTON HARBOR OBJECTS

Solution on page 68

TEA

MOUNT RUSHMORE NATIONAL MEMORIAL

BLACK HILLS, SOUTH DAKOTA

Built from 1927-1941 there are sculpted 60-foot-tall heads of four United States presidents: George Washington, Thomas Jefferson, Theodore Roosevelt, and Abraham Lincoln (left to right) representing the nation's birth, growth, development, and preservation.

FIND 12 MOUNTAIN ANIMALS & PLANTS

Solution on page 69

CASA GRANDE RUINS NATIONAL MONUMENT

COOLIDGE, ARIZONA

Casa Grande Ruins are Pre-Columbian ruins in south-central Arizona. Named Casa Grande Ruins Reservation in 1889, the 0.7 square mile site was designated as a national monument in 1918. Built by Salado Indians, a Pueblo people, in the early 14th century, it has four stories. Openings in the walls align with the sun & moon at different times during the year.

FIND 12 DESERT PLANTS

Solution on page 69

CLASSIC AMERICAN WORKING FARM

American Farm Bureau Federation, the largest farmers' organization in the United States, founded in 1919, is an independent nongovernmental federation of farm bureaus from all 50 states and Puerto Rico. It advocates for farm and ranch families on issues & topics impacting agriculture.

FIND 12 FARM ANIMALS

Solution on page 69

THE BROOKLYN BRIDGE

MANHATTAN & BROOKLYN, NEW YORK

The_Brooklyn Bridge was called the eighth wonder of the world when it opened on May 24, 1883. It spans the East River between Manhattan and Brooklyn and was the first steel cable suspension bridge & the longest suspension bridge in the world at the time of its completion.

FIND 12 THINGS ON OR NEAR A BRIDGE

Solution on page 69

27

GATEWAY ARCH
ST. LOUIS, MISSOURI

Gateway Arch National Park, formerly Jefferson National Expansion Memorial, was founded by the National Park Service in 1935 to commemorate Thomas Jefferson's vision of a transcontinental United States. Completed in 1965, the Gateway Arch rising 630 feet, is a bold monument to the pioneering spirit of the diverse people who shaped the country.

FIND 12 SIGNS

Solution on page 70

DINNER
ONE WAY
TIME
-to-
EAT
STOP
SNACKS
ICE CREAM
FRESH DONUTS
here
PIZZA MENU
BAKERY
Pop corn
cookies

INDEPENDENCE HALL & THE LIBERTY BELL

PHILADELPHIA. PENNSYLVANIA

The Declaration of Independence & the Constitution were debated and adopted by America's Founding Fathers in Independence Hall. Completed in 1753, it was the first capitol of the United States & where the US Constitution was ratified, The Liberty Bell, which cracked when first rung after its arrival in Philadelphia, was in the steeple of Independence Hall, but is now across the street.

FIND 12 AMERICAN ICONS

We the People

Solution on page 70

freedom
We the People

FISHERMAN'S WHARF

SAN FRANCISCO, CALIFORNIA

Historic Fisherman's Wharf, on the northern waterfront, blends old and new. It's a busy tourist area but it is still the fishing fleet operated by 3rd & 4th generations of fishermen that helps the wharf remain the center of ocean-oriented activity. There are also amazing views of the bay, Golden Gate and Alcatraz, a colony of sea lions, and historic ships.

FIND THE 12 FISH

Solution on page 70

MONUMENT VALLEY NAVAHO TRIBAL PARK

NAVAHO NATION, UTAH

Located in the heart of the Navajo Nation the valley is considered to be a sacred place in traditional Navajo culture. The name refers to towering buttes and spires rising out of the desert which are called monuments. In the Navajo language it is Tsé Bii' Ndzisgaii, or "The Valley of the Rocks."

FIND 12 DESERT ITEMS

Solution on page 70

FENWAY PARK
BOSTON, MASSACHUSETTS

Fenway Park, the baseball park in Boston, is home to the Red Sox. It opened in 1912 and is the oldest stadium in Major League Baseball and one of its most famous. The Green Monster is a popular nickname for the 37-foot-2-inch high left field wall.

FIND 12 STADIUM DRINKS & SNACKS

Solution on page 71

FENWAY

CAPE HENRY LIGHTHOUSE

FORT STORY, VIRGINIA

The original Cape Henry Lighthouse is the 4th oldest lighthouse in the US and the first lighthouse authorized by the US government in 1792. The lighthouse helps protect & guide vessels entering and leaving Chesapeake Bay. Another lighthouse, still functional, was built next to it in 1881.

FIND THE 12 SEASHELLS

Solution on page 71

USS ARIZONA MEMORIAL
PEARL HARBOR, HAWAII

The memorial marks the resting place of 1,102 of the 1,177 sailors and Marines killed on the USS Arizona during the attack on Pearl Harbor on December 7, 1941 which led to US involvement in World War II.

FIND 12 STARS

Solution on page 71

USS Arizona

TIMES SQUARE

NEW YORK CITY

Times Square is one of the most visited places in the world with about 50 million visitors a year. Originally Longacre Square it was renamed Times Square when the NY Times moved to Times Tower on the square in 1904. It is a crowded, vibrant, exciting center for entertainment and theater.

FIND 12 FRIENDLY MONSTERS

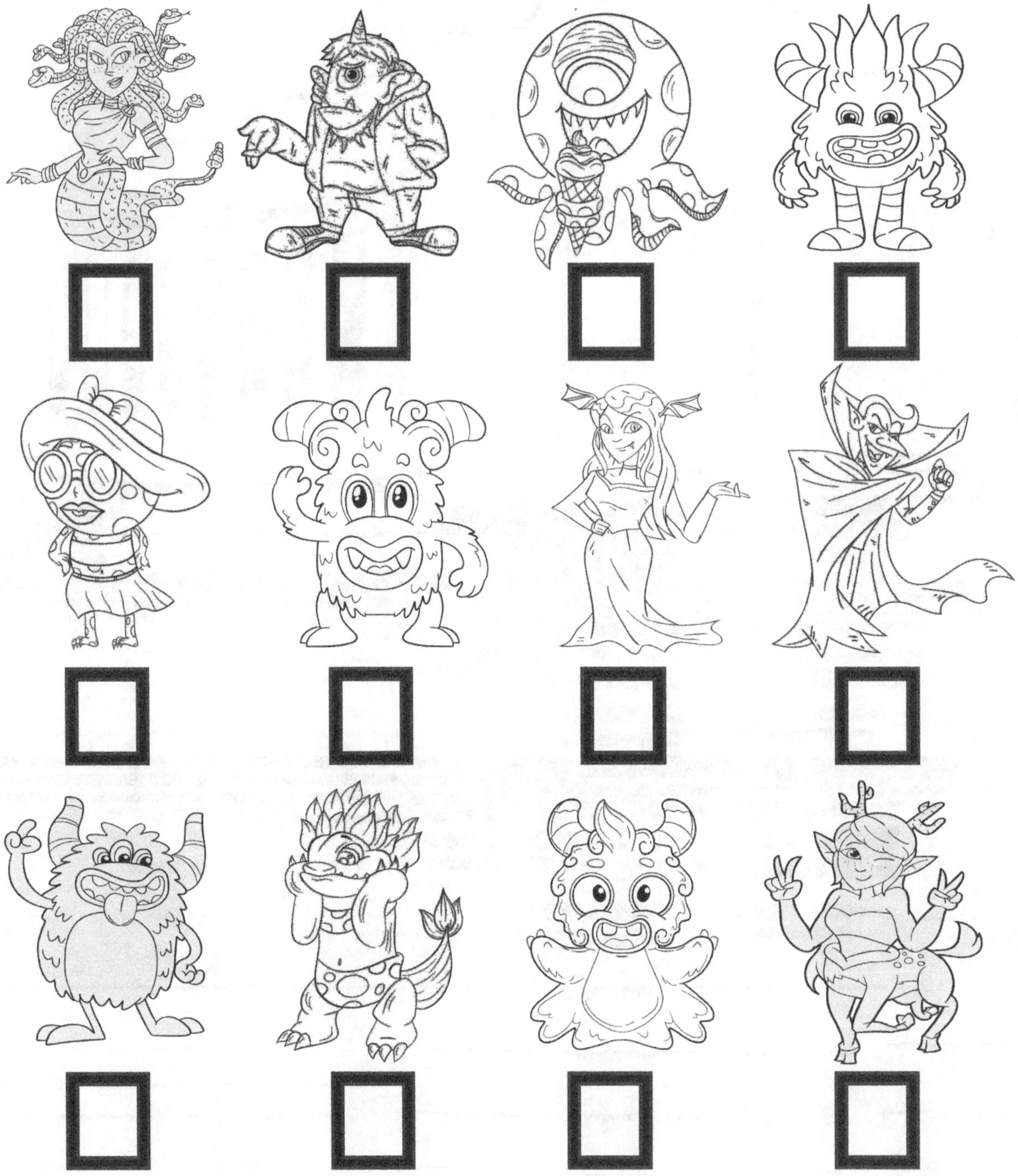

Solution on page 71

CONEY ISLAND

BROOKLYN, NEW YORK

Coney Island is known for its iconic Riegelmann boardwalk. It's over 100 years old and stretches approximately 2.7 miles along the magnificent sandy beach and rolling waves of the Atlantic Ocean. It is also home to an aquarium, action-packed rides, restaurants, shops, businesses and a residential community. Food abounds and famous rides in Luna Park include the Wonder Wheel ferris wheel, the Parachute jump and the Cyclone roller coaster.

FIND 12 BEACH & BOARDWALK OBJECTS

Solution on page 72

WONDER WHEEL

THE ALAMO
SAN ANTONIO, TEXAS

The Alamo, an 18th-century former Fanciscan mission in San Antonio, was the site, in 1836, of a famous resistance effort by small group of determined fighters for Texan independence from Mexico. The Texans held off the Mexicans for 13 days but the Mexicans overwhelmed the Texans. Almost all the defenders, including Davy Crockett, died.

FIND 12 OBJECTS AROUND THE ALAMO

Solution on page 72

GRAND CANYON NATIONAL PARK
ARIZONA

The Grand Canyon is a huge and deep canyon created, starting about six million years ago, by the Colorado River running through it. Located in the high plateau region of northwestern Arizona, it dazzles with fantastic colors and shapes. The Grand Canyon begins in the Northeast near the town of Page, Arizona and continues west for 277 miles.

12 PIECES OF CAMPING EQUIPMENT

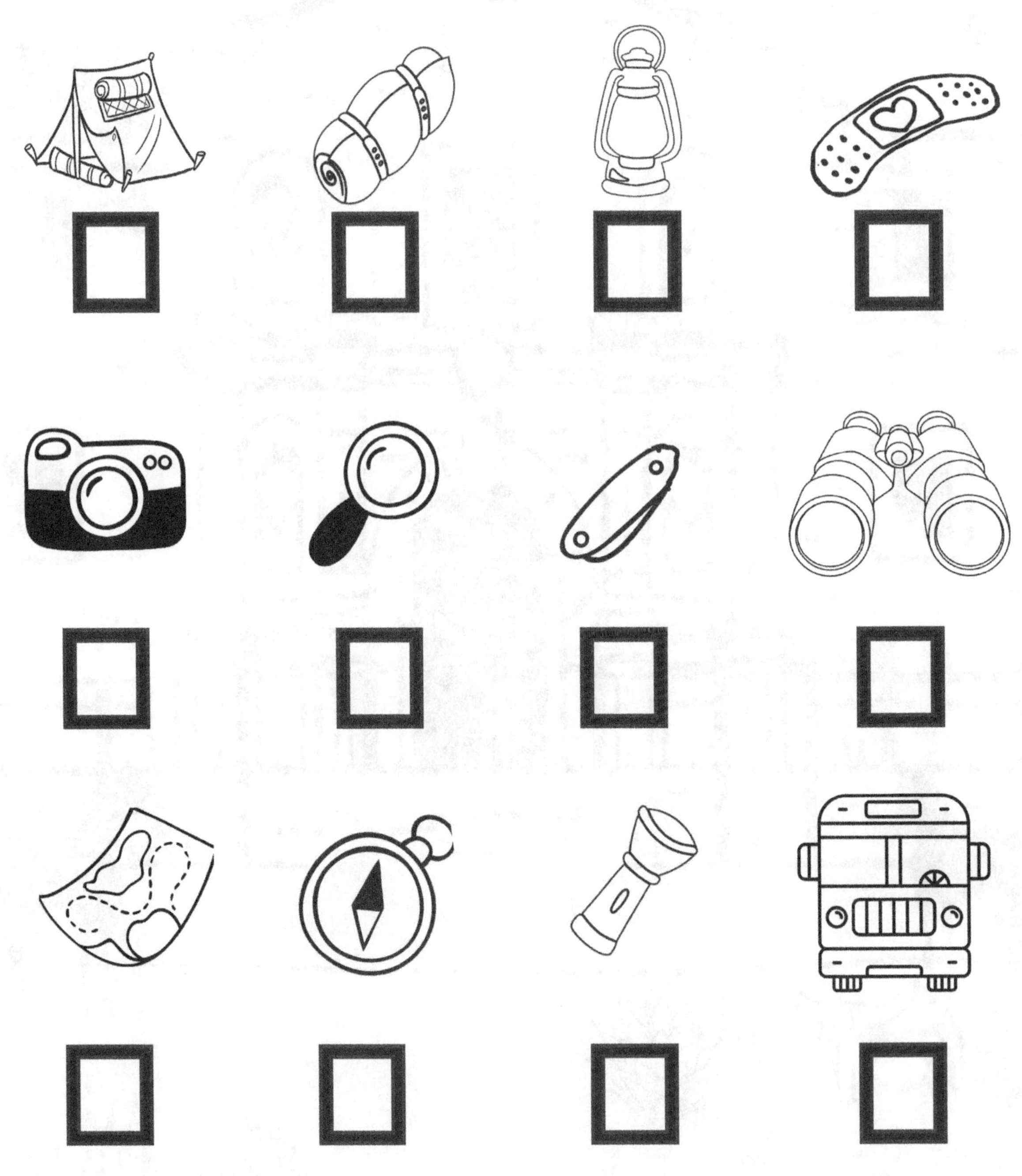

Solution on page 72

LINCOLN MEMORIAL

WASHINGTON DC

The 16th president, Lincoln is famous for many things including the Emancipation Proclamation (1863), Gettysburg Address (1863) and passage of the 13th Amendment (ratified 1865), which outlawed slavery. The memorial, which includes the reflecting pool, symbolizes his belief in the dignity and freedom of all people and honors him and "the virtues of tolerance, honesty, and constancy in the human spirit."

FIND 12 ITEMS AROUND THE MONUMENT

Solution on page 72

FOUR
SCORE
AND SEVEN
YEARD AGO

BOURBON STREET

NEW ORLEANS, LOUISIANA

The historic street in the heart of the French Quarter of New Orleans dates to 1721. A French engineer laid out the streets of New Orleans and named Bourbon Street after name of the ruling French royal family. The street is raucous, nocturnal and party central. New Orleans is the birthplace of jazz and music can be heard all along Bourbon Street.

FIND 12 OBJECTS RELATED TO MUSIC

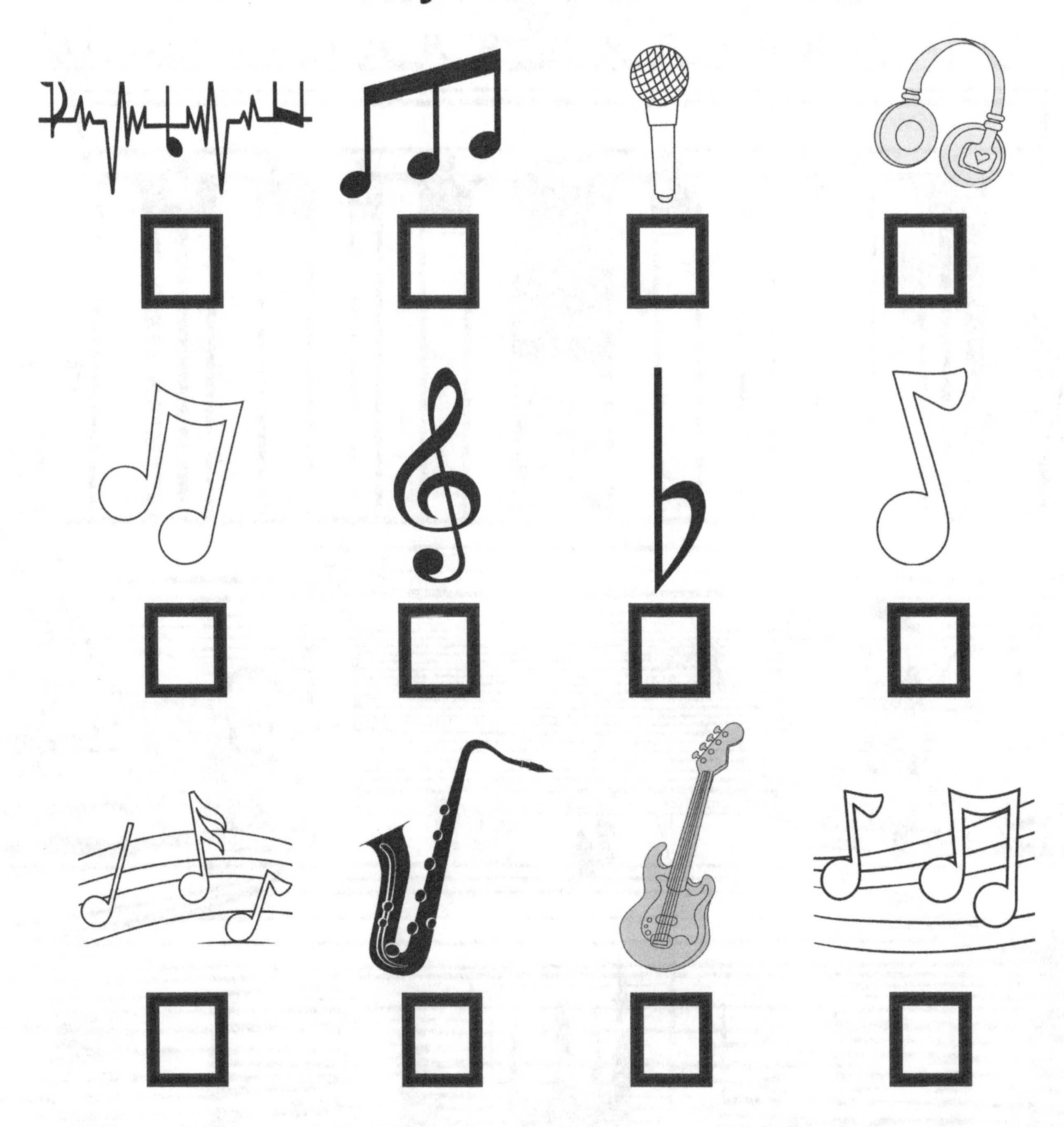

Solution on page 73

ALCATRAZ ISLAND

SAN FRANCISCO, CALIFORNIA

A small island 1.25 miles offshore from San Francisco, it was developed in the mid-19th century with a still operational lighthouse, a military fortification, and a military prison. In 1934 the island was converted into a federal prison. Strong currents & cold water temperatures made escape nearly impossible & the prison became one of the most notorious in US history. It closed in 1963 the island is now a tourist attraction.

FIND 12 WATER ANIMALS

Solution on page 73

ELLIS ISLAND
NEW YORK HARBOR

Ellis Island began receiving immigrants on January 1, 1892. Over the next 62 years more than 12 million people, many of them Russians, Italians, Slavs, Jews, Greeks, Poles, Serbs & Turks from southern & eastern Europe were given permission to enter the US. Located near Liberty Island, it's now home to the Ellis Island National Museum of Immigration.

FIND 12 FLAGS & ARRIVAL ITEMS

Solution on page 73

SPACE NEEDLE

SEATTLE, WASHINGTON

Officially opened to the public on April 21, 1962 for the Century 21 Exposition, a space-themed World's Fair, it was named s landmark in 1999. There are 360-degree views from its three main viewing areas and The Loupe, the world's first revolving glass floor, was installed in 2018.

FIND 12 TRANSPORTATION ITEMS

Solution on page 73

HOOVER DAM
NEVADA & ARIZONA

Located on the border between Nevada and Arizona it is named after President Herbert Hoover. Construction began in 1931 and took five years to complete. 726 feet tall and is 1,244 feet long, it was built to provide irrigation water and hydroelectric power and to control seasonal flooding of the Colorado River making downstream settlement possible.

FIND 12 OBJECTS SEEN NEAR A DAM

Solution on page 74

METROPOLITAN MUSEUM OF ART

NEW YORK CITY

One of the world's finest and largest art museums, its collections include 1.5 million works of art spanning 5,000 years of world culture from every part of the globe. Located on Manhattan's Museum mile it extends into Central Park.

FIND 12 OBJECTS FOUND NEAR A CITY MUSEUM

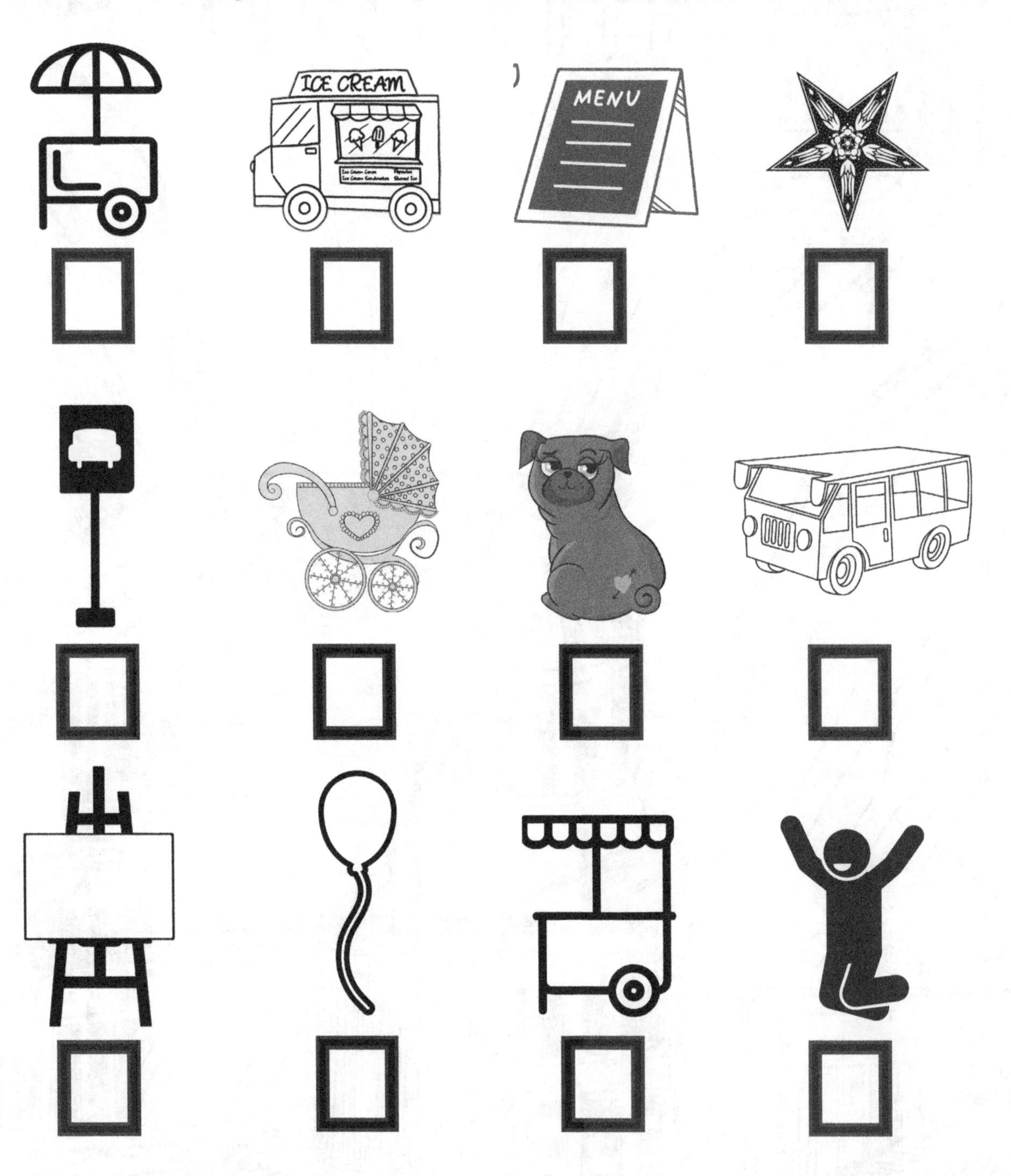

Solution on page 74

TAXI
MENU
ICE CREAM

UNITED STATES MILITARY ACADEMY
WEST POINT, NEW YORK

The United States Military Academy is the oldest American service academy and educates cadets for commissioning into the US Army. Originally established as a fort during the Revolutionary War, it sits on strategic high ground overlooking the Hudson River 50 miles north of New York City. It is the oldest continuously occupied military post in the United States.

FIND 12 PATRIOTIC & MILITARY OBJECTS

Solution on page 74

SOLUTIONS

Statue of Liberty

Yosemite

Farmhouse Kitchen

Hollywood

Las Vegas

Portland Head Light

Niagara Falls

Boston Harbor

Mount Rushmore

Casa Grande

American Farm

Brooklyn Bridge

Gateway Arch

Liberty Bell

Fisherman's Wharf

Monument Valley

Fenway

Cape Henry

USS Arizona

Times Square

Coney Island

The Alamo

Grand Canyon

Lincoln Memorial

Bourbon Street

Alcatraz

Ellis Island

Space Needle

Hoover Dam

Metropolitan Museum

West Point

We hope you enjoyed our book. Please check out the other puzzle and activity books by Copper Penny Puzzles® listed on Amazon.

We are a small independent publisher and would very much appreciate it if you would take the time to leave a a positive review on Amazon.

Thanks very much.

OTHER BOOKS FROM COPPER PENNY PUZZLES

https://amzn.to/38A18b6

https://amzn.to/3twP1mL

https://amzn.to/3Qk5UdD

https://amzn.to/48w7L8r

https://amzn.to/3WXFC4q

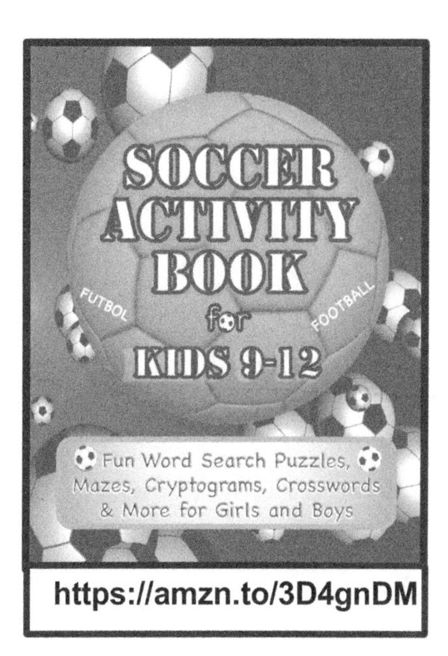

https://amzn.to/3D4gnDM

https://amzn.to/3fQTcG0

https://amzn.to/3G0QI2w

Made in the USA
Las Vegas, NV
09 July 2024